ISBN:978-1-7782386-0-4
Published:2022

Believe !
All Things Are Possible.

Written by Tashana Swaby-Scott

To every child reading this book....

continue to believe!

Do you believe?

Believe what? Kavia.

"Believe that I can win this contest and get to go to science camp and meet HER." Kavia sits on a rock by the seaside, looking deep into the sky as if she entered another world.

Caleb turned to look at Kavia as if she was mad and replied, "of course, I believe you can win; we have practiced every day. We might not have the right equipment, but one thing I know is that I BELIEVE."

"This is where all our dreams can come true. Great things can happen right here in our neighbourhood, look at the ocean, isn't beautiful ? People just need to believe and have a little imagination, so many wonderful things can happen."

"You have lots of imagination Caleb; you are always dreaming of adventures, beautiful places, and people. How come you are always dreaming of those things?" Kavia asked.

Caleb sat beside Kavia with his back leaned against the rock he said, "Kavia, I see beautiful places in my dreams, and I believe that one day I will get there. Or maybe it's because I can imagine them that's why I believe; I am not too sure, but I know that I believe."

I believe all things are possible, even right here in Waterview. The people here can't see the beauty in this place and all the greatness it has because they don't believe. They talk all the time about how alive our neighbourhood was, but they don't seem to believe it can happen again.

I believe that we were all born with love. I believe that everything is possible, but we can't have what we want or need if we do not believe that we can have it. So just as we talk about things every day, we must work on our dreams too. I know we can't just dream and believe we must work too.

Kavia jumped to her feet as if she was just given a new life. She said "So it makes no sense talking and talking if I don't believe."

"No, I don't think so; we all need to have a little faith. Ask, believe, work at it, and our dreams will come true." Caleb replied.

"I know in my heart that one day Waterview is going to be the best neighbourhood in our city, where people will cook, laugh, sing and dance again," said Caleb.

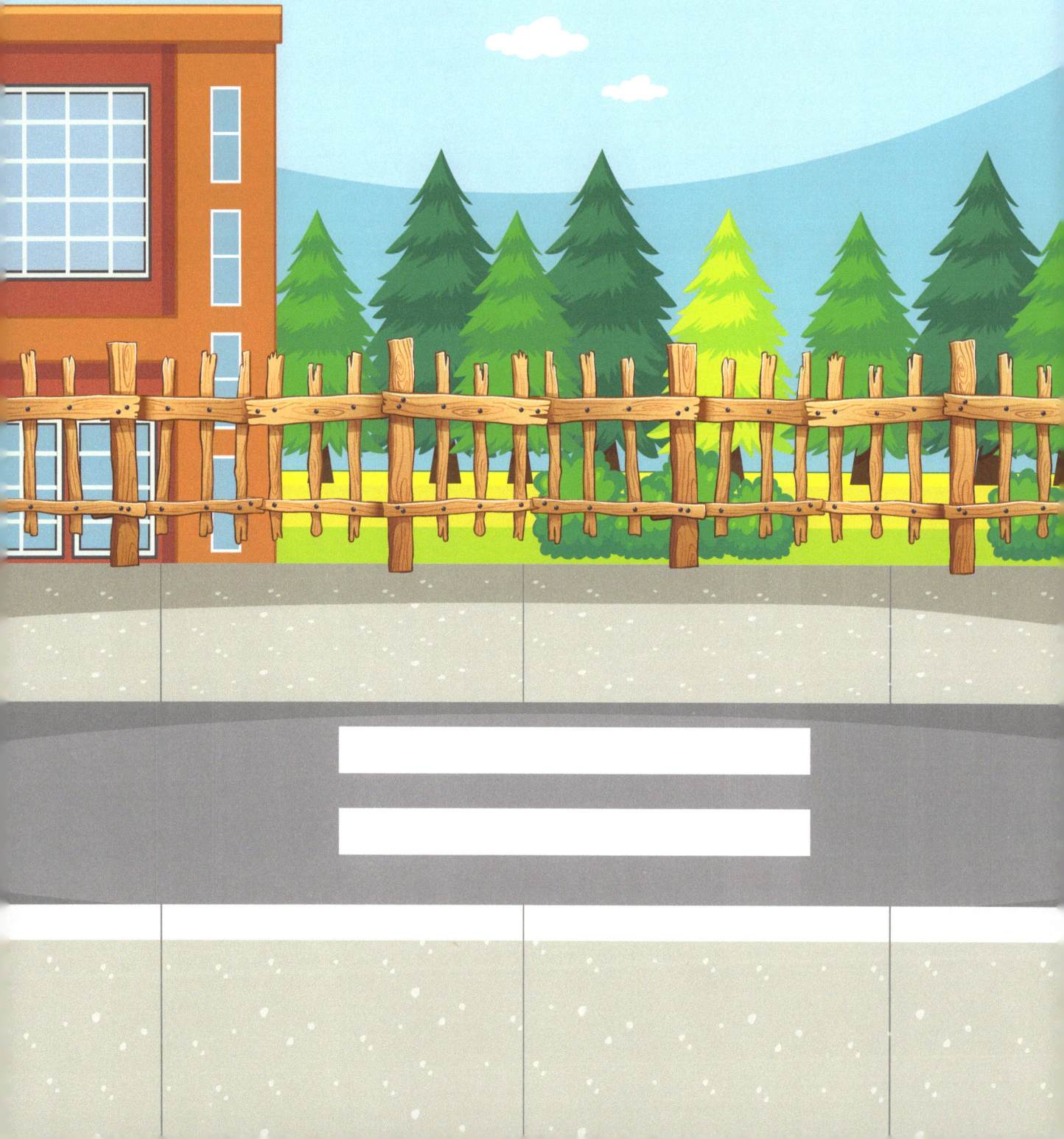

"People will come from all over the world to see our neighbourhood and eat lots of juicy lobster and crab legs..."Caleb said and they both laughed. "Caleb, you are always thinking about food; everything must come back to food." Kavia said chuckling.

"But Kavia can you see it? Can you feel what I am talking about? Everything we need is right here, and it's inside of us."

Beauty is everywhere; it's not just one place, it's everywhere, the beauty that you seek is already here. The change you want is already here.

It is inside of you; we are the change, we can make great things happen.

To make things happen, we just need a little faith, and every other thing will be added along the way.

Kavia looked at him with a strange look as if she was trying to understand how was Caleb so wise. She said, "Caleb for an 8 year old, you are sounding like you have lived for 50 years."

"No! it's just 8 years with my granny," he said with a belly laugh. Kavia laughed so hard as well that she had to stop and catch her breath.

"Listening to my grandmother every day makes me wiser." (He smiles but with a kind of seriousness as if to ensure she knows that he believes in everything he said.)

"I hear you, Caleb." Kavia said

I believe I can....

The next day Caleb went to Kavia's house to help her get her project ready. "Are you ready to help me Caleb?" "Yeah, let's go." replied Caleb.

He played music on his phone while Kavia mixed her ingredients, a little bit of this and a little bit of that, and a whole lot of things that he did not recognize.

She worked on her project with deep focus; after all, she needed to win this contest. Children from three of the other neighbourhoods in the city would be competing for the grand prize; to visit the most famous science center in the country.

If she won she would get to meet her favourite scientist and get to attend summer camp.

Kavia had always dreamt of going to one of these summer camps, but never thought she would get to meet her favourite scientist and an opportunity to go to the best science centre in the country.

As she completed her mixtures, she turned to him and gave a bow as if she had completed a masterpiece.

On the day of the contest, Kavia was nervous; she had all sorts of thoughts racing through her mind.

She nervously said, "Caleb, what if I trip and fall flat on my face in front of everyone, what if I forget the formula? what if...."

"Kavia, snap out of it" he said, "remember you have put in the work; now all you have to do is give it your all and believe!"

Just before it became her time to present her work, Kavia took a moment backstage and whispered to herself, "I believe, I believe, I believe."

She went on stage and her eyes met with her best friend, Caleb whispered, "believe.... you can do this."

She moved her hands as if there was no one watching, putting a little bit of this and a little bit of that. Her hands moved as if she was making a musical rhythm. She finally finished her presentation, and what a presentation it was.

Kavia won first place; she did it; not only did she put in the work she also believed in herself, and her dream had finally become a reality. To her surprise, her neighbourhood also won a chance to be on national television.

She thought, people from all over the country would come and visit. This would give the people of Waterview a chance to cook and have booths to show their craft, music, and dance. Waterview would come alive again.

"Caleb, Caleb did you hear that? It is going to happen, just as you said. People will come to see our town, eat lobsters, dance, and sing."

"Of course, I heard, I knew it would happen one day, I knew Waterview would come alive again." He said with a big grin on his face.

"I believe Caleb, I believe with all my heart that dreams can come true. Thank you for believing in me Caleb"

What do you believe?...

Kavia and Caleb ran off to their homes, jumping and skipping with excitement making their way through the garden. There is power in belief. Beautiful, magnificent things can happen when we believe.

All things are possible!

www.ingramcontent.com/pod-product-compliance
Lightning Source LLC
LaVergne TN
LVHW072056070426

835508LV00002B/126